Consultant, Istar Schwager, holds a Ph.D. in educational psychology
and a master's degree in early childhood education.
She has been an advisor, consultant, and content designer for numerous parenting,
child development, and early learning programs including the *Sesame Street*
television show and magazines.
She has been a consultant for several Fortune 500 companies
and has regularly published articles for parents
on a range of topics.

Louis Weber, C.E.O.
Publications International, Ltd.
7373 North Cicero Avenue
Lincolnwood, Illinois 60646

Manufactured in the U.S.A.

8 7 6 5 4 3 2

ISBN 1-56173-485-3

active minds

alphabet

PHOTOGRAPHY
George Siede and Donna Preis

CONSULTANT
Istar Schwager, Ph.D.

Publications
International,
Ltd.

A

A is for **apple**, **B** is for **bunny**,

B

c is for clown. Isn't he funny?

C

A B C

D is for **d**og,

D

E

E is for **e**ggs,

F

F is for **five** frogs with green legs.

A B C D E F

G is for glasses, H is for hat,

G

H

I

is for ice cream. Who doesn't like that?

A B C D E F G H I

J

J is for **jacket**, **K** is for **kitten**,

K

L is for lemon, **M** is for mitten.

M

L

A B C D E F G H I J K L M

N

N is for **n**oodles,

O

O is for an **o**range treat,

A B C

P

P is for **p**uzzle,

Put together nice and neat.

D E F G H I J K L M N O P

Q is for **quilt**, **R** is for **rain**,

A B C D E F G

S O

S is for **seashells**, **T** is for **train**.

T

H I J K L M N O P Q R S T

U V

U is for umbrella, V is for violin,

A B C D E F G H I J

W is for a wagon that you can ride in.

W

K L M N O P Q R S T U V W

X is for **x**ylophone, **Y** is for **yo-yo**,

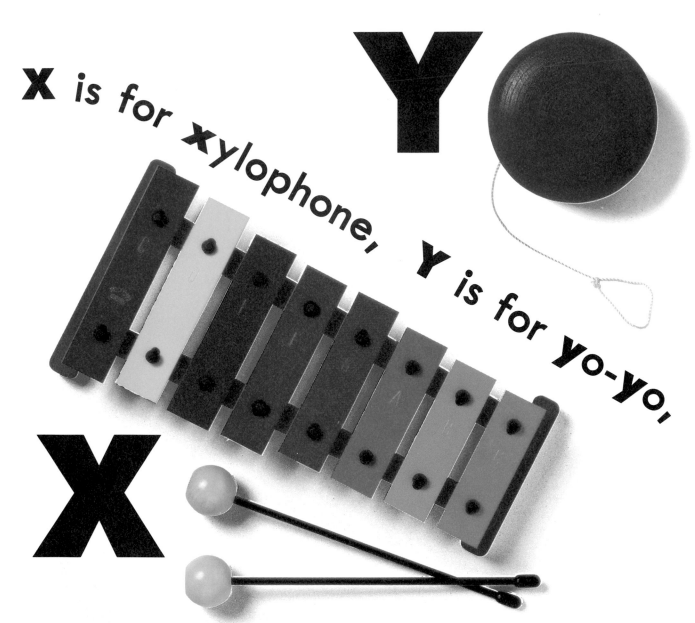

Y

X

A B C D E F G H I J K L M

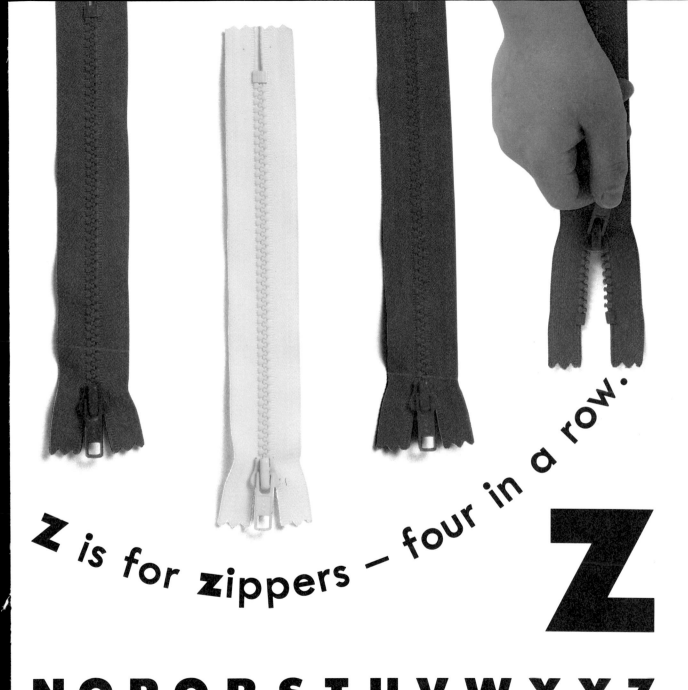

Z is for zippers – four in a row.

Z

NOPQRSTUVWXYZ